PUGWASH

ALSO BY VERN THIESSEN

The Courier and Other Plays
Einstein's Gift
Of Human Bondage
Shakespeare's Will
Vimy

PUGWASH

VERN THIESSEN

PLAYWRIGHTS CANADA PRESS
TORONTO

For professional or amateur production rights, please contact:
Michael Petrasek at Kensington Literary Representation
34 St. Andrew Street, Toronto, ON M5T 1K6
416.848.9648, kensingtonlit@rogers.com

LIBRARY AND ARCHIVES CANADA CATALOGUING IN PUBLICATION
Title: Pugwash / Vern Thiessen.
Names: Thiessen, Vern, author.
Description: First edition. | A play.
Identifiers: Canadiana (print) 20190195029
| Canadiana (ebook) 20190195045 | ISBN 9780369100603 (softcover)
| ISBN 9780369100610 (PDF) | ISBN 9780369100627 (EPUB)
| ISBN 9780369100634 (Kindle)
Classification: LCC PS8589.H4524 P84 2019 | DDC C812/.54—dc23

Playwrights Canada Press acknowledges that we operate on land, which, for thousands of years, has been the traditional territories of the Mississaugas of the Credit, Huron-Wendat, Anishinaabe, Métis, and Haudenosaunee peoples. Today, this meeting place is home to many Indigenous peoples from across Turtle Island and we are grateful to have the opportunity to work and play here.

We acknowledge the financial support of the Canada Council for the Arts—which last year invested $153 million to bring the arts to Canadians throughout the country—the Ontario Arts Council (OAC), Ontario Creates, and the Government of Canada for our publishing activities.

Canada Council for the Arts | Conseil des arts du Canada

ONTARIO ARTS COUNCIL
CONSEIL DES ARTS DE L'ONTARIO
an Ontario government agency
un organisme du gouvernement de l'Ontario

Canada

ONTARIO CREATES | ONTARIO CRÉATIF

For Ethan and Milo. Their future is in our hands.

PREFACE

This play is a work of fiction based on historical events. The first Pugwash conference happened in July 1957. The characters of Ogawa and Alex are based on scientists who were indeed there and housed as described in the play. To this day, scientists are often housed in Pugwashians' homes. It has become a tradition. The tension between Ogawa and Alex is purely fictional, though the history between their countries of origin is based on fact. I believe these characters would have been aware of this. The conference was broken into several sessions, including the Responsibility of the Scientist and the Effects of Radiation. However, the speeches given in the play are my adaptation of what was spoken. Cyrus Eaton did indeed host the conference. However, he did not chair any of the sessions, preferring to leave the scientists to have their discussions in private. Brown is a fictional creation based on certain right-wing American writers that were in the pocket of the CIA at the time, under a program called Operation Mockingbird. Reporters were allowed limited access to the conference, and many major newspapers, including the *New York Times*, sent reporters. Brown is my own way of bringing the political pressures of the time into the play: on governments, scientists, and on Eaton, who was viewed dimly by the right-wing conservative press for his dealings with the Soviet Union. The town of

Pugwash has indeed been plagued by an inordinate number of fires that have destroyed the town repeatedly. Of course, there was no fire during the first conference, but it wouldn't have been a surprise if there was.

The child characters in the play are composites based on many people I spoke to in Pugwash, who kindly shared their memories of those first early years of the Pugwash conferences.

It took me a long time to write this play. The Pugwash conferences, like the town, are filled with such lore, and with such a rich array of "characters" it was challenging to find a way to portray it on the stage. "How do I tell this story?" I asked myself over and over again. Is Joseph Rotblat the hero of this story, having quit the Manhattan Project? Is Cyrus Eaton the hero for hosting the conference? Is Anne—Cyrus Eaton's future wife—the hero, as she was really the social coordinator of the conference? How do I portray the scientists' discussions in a dramatic way, when by all accounts the discussions were very civil and drama free? Do I try and put twenty-two scientists on the stage and break the theatre's bank account? Do I place only the villagers of Pugwash on the stage and get them to act out the story of the first conference? How do I paint a backdrop of the Cold War in a small fishing village? How do I honour the work of the men and women of the village and those visiting "thinkers" without simply making things up?

I have written five plays that involve historical events and real persons. And every time I've searched for the untold story. I have always followed Aristotle's dictum that "history is what actually happened; drama is what might have happened." There are enough books, articles, and documentaries on Sir Joseph Rotblat and Cyrus Eaton to last a lifetime. There are wiki articles on almost every scientist who has been to the conference. There are enough memories and anecdotes from townspeople to fill the Pugwash archives. But what's the *untold* story? Who are the central characters we know little about, or who have never been part of the picture? And why am I writing this play in the first place? After five years, and several failed drafts, I remembered something.

When I first went to Pugwash for the conference in 2012, I was particularly struck by one event. A scientist was billeted with a family—as they still are—in a house across from Thinkers' Lodge. There was a girl living in the house. Her name was Billie. She was very shy. And at the end of the three days she presented the scientist with a painting she had made. When Billie was encouraged, somewhat reluctantly, to show her art to the conference on the final evening, the room fell silent. It was a painting depicting her fears of nuclear disaster. It was moving and poignant. It reminded me—and, I believe, all people present—that art is our mirror, telescope, looking glass, and kaleidoscope, all in one. A child painted a picture that said everything that needed to be said. A child took action; she took responsibility for the world she knew in one of the few ways available to her.

I hope this play does that child justice.

—Vern Thiessen

P.S. There are many things that are killing our planet and its inhabitants (animals, minerals, and vegetables) slowly. And humans are collectively responsible for this. There are also things that can kill the planet very quickly, with the push of a button and by a very small group of people. We are also collectively responsible for this.

Pugwash was commissioned by the Ensemble Studio Theatre (New York City) and the Alfred P. Sloan Foundation. It was developed with the assistance of the Ensemble Studio Theatre, Alberta Playwrights' Network, the Playwrights Guild of Canada, and Ship's Company Theatre (Parrsboro, Nova Scotia). The play premiered at Ship's Company Theatre on July 5, 2017, with the following cast and creative team:

Brown: Karen Bassett
Cyrus Eaton: Stephen Cross
Jamie: Henricus Gielis
Ogawa: Ian Leung
Alex: Theo Pitsiavas
Conni: Gina Thornhill

Director: Natasha MacLellan
Set Designer: Garrett Barker
Lighting Designer: Vicky Williams
Costume Designer: Cathleen McCormick
Sound Designer: Paul Del Motte
Stage Managers: Ingrid Risk and Hannah Burrows
Apprentice Stage Manager: Carmen Lee
Production Manager and Technical Director: Justin Dakai
Head Carpenter: Jonah Lerner
Assistant Carpenter: Jess Preece
Technician: Trent Logan

CHARACTERS

Conni: In the present, a woman in her mid-seventies. In the past, a girl of about thirteen years old.
Jamie: A boy, about eleven years old.
Ogawa: A Japanese scientist, about forty years old.
Alex: A Soviet scientist, about fifty years old.
Brown: A reporter, in his thirties.
Cyrus Eaton: A wealthy industrialist, in his sixties.

SETTING

The play takes place in Conni's memory. The main action takes place in early July 1957, in Pugwash, Nova Scotia.

This play is a piece of theatre. Actors should be cast regardless of age, gender, or physical ability.

The break at the end of Act One is optional.

ACT ONE

CONNI speaks to the audience.

CONNI: The sunrise here is always quiet.

Have you noticed that?

It rises soft and slow.
Gliding over Fox Harbour like a gull.
Floating past the Lower Gulf Shore like a big red balloon.
Easing over Matheson's Cove like a breeze.
Waking us all up.
Again.

She sighs, restless.

This place, this place.

So small, it slides off a map.
So empty, there're more streets than people.
Why would they come here?
Why would they come to a place of shallow, warm water.
When the war they were fighting was so deep and cold?

JAMIE appears. He's been there all along in the shadows of her memory.

He hauls two bundles of newspapers. He sets one down and stands on it, holding aloft a copy. This is now the post office steps.

And here you are. Jamie Gillis.
Your face, red as the lighthouse on Pugwash Point.
Your lanky hands, blackened from newsprint.
Your eleven-year-old heart full of fire.

JAMIE: FI-RE!

CONNI: July 4th, 1957. Pugwash, Nova Scotia.

JAMIE: READ ALL ABOUT IT! RAGING FIRE ONCE MORE STRIKES THE TOWN OF PUGWASH, NOVA SCOTIA! FI-RE!

CONNI is thirteen years old now.

CONNI: For Pete's sake, Jamie Gillis! Stop that! What in the devil's name do you think you're doing?

JAMIE: What's it look like? I'm crying the news.

CONNI: The news? Hanging onto the post office steps, hollering "fire" to the dirt road, when it's obvious there IS no fire.

JAMIE: It's my job to sell the *Amherst Daily News*, Conni McPhee. And a good fire always sells a newspaper.

CONNI: If people were listening! Do you see anyone down Prince Albert Street there? No. And do you see anyone coming up Water Street here? No. You know why? They're WORKING. They're out fishing and farming and doing what they need to make a living.

JAMIE: What are you doing here then?

CONNI: My daddy's running the mail, fool!

JAMIE: I thought your daddy was working the mill.

CONNI: He was, until he got the asthma.

JAMIE: I thought Mr. Deekan was running the mail.

CONNI: Deekan's helping Old Man Mundle at the funeral home.

JAMIE: Why's Mundle need help at the funeral home?

CONNI: His wife died.

JAMIE: Deekan's?

CONNI: NO, MUNDLE'S! So Deekan's helping him out with the dead.

JAMIE: His wife?

CONNI: The OTHER dead. And that means Daddy's running the mail.

JAMIE: Why's your daddy not helping Mundle with the dead so Deekan can still do the mail?

CONNI: My daddy doesn't know nothing about preparing the dead!

JAMIE: But—

CONNI: If you spent half the amount of time listening to what's going on in Pugwash as you do crying the news to crows on the post office steps, you'd know what I was talking about.

JAMIE: That still doesn't answer why you're here when your daddy's out running the mail.

CONNI: Bringing him LUNCH.

She holds up the lunch.

Satisfied?

She sits down on the steps. She takes out a sketchbook and pencil crayons. She draws.

JAMIE: What you got there?

CONNI: Sketchbook and pencils. Eaton's catalogue.

JAMIE: What you gonna draw?

CONNI: Cat.

JAMIE: You don't have a cat.

CONNI: Don't have to have a cat to draw one.

He stands and shouts:

JAMIE: FI-RE, FI-RE!

CONNI: For Pete's sake, Jamie. Stop yellin' like that or you're going to end up like one of those drunks in front of the Tide's Inn.

JAMIE: I'm a paper boy, what else am I supposed to do?

CONNI: Deliver your newspapers, for a start.

JAMIE: Only got seventeen customers. Was done two hours ago.

CONNI: Well then how about crying what's actually NEWS.

JAMIE: The past's always more interesting than the present, Conni. That's what they call "history." Look at Halifax. It's what it is because of the explosion. Look at Rome. It's interesting because of what happened to it, not because of what it is today. It burned while Nero fiddled, that's what Miss Alison taught us. You wanna be the one fiddling while Pugwash burns?

CONNI: What is it with you and fires.

JAMIE: Are you kidding me? Pugwash, with only eight hundred souls, has seen six major fires. Six! We have to be vigilant, Conni. We can't forget our history. Which is why I keep a stack of every edition of the *Amherst Daily News* I can find in the shed behind the post office. An archives, they call it.

CONNI: A lot of work for nothing.

JAMIE: All great places have archives to store their memory. And Pugwash is gonna be a great place. It's gonna be famous.

CONNI: Ha! For what? Canning lobster?

JAMIE: For this. Right here. You want news? I'll tell you.

He unfolds the newspaper. CY *and* BROWN *appear.*

(reads) "Thinkers Coming to Pugwash."

CONNI: Thinkers?

BROWN: Mr. Eaton! Mr. Eaton!

JAMIE: "Twenty-two Thinkers from around the world will be descending on the village of Pugwash for three days to discuss the perils of nuclear war."

CY: Scientists from countries including the Soviet Union, Japan, Germany, Australia, the United States, China, and the United Kingdom will be present for the first meeting of its kind in the world.

JAMIE: "The scientists are here at the invitation of wealthy Cleveland industrialist and pride of Pugwash, Cyrus Eaton."

CONNI/BROWN: Why do scientists need to come/go to Pugwash to think?

JAMIE: I dunno.

CY: These men need a place where they may discuss the possible dangers of radiation testing and the realities of nuclear war surrounded by beauty and peace, without the distractions a city brings with it.

CY and BROWN vanish.

CONNI: *(not impressed)* Cy Eaton.

JAMIE: Don't be saying a bad word about Cyrus Eaton.

CONNI: *(dismissively)* Him and his fancy car up from Cleveland.

JAMIE: Cy Eaton walked down our street one morning and he gave me some licorice. He's promising to pave the roads in Pugwash.

CONNI: The day.

JAMIE: AND build a school.

CONNI: What we need another school for?

JAMIE: Cuz they keep BURNING DOWN!

CONNI: Och.

JAMIE: Makes a fortune, loses it in the Depression, then makes it all back tenfold. Hauling water at six and a billionaire at sixty!

CONNI: Always "puttin' on the dog," that's what Daddy says about Cy Eaton.

JAMIE: Your daddy.

CONNI: Don't you say anything 'bout my daddy, Jamie Gillis, or I'll pop you. My daddy milled the wood for most of the houses in this town, and his daddy before him.

JAMIE: Course he did. With all the fires, there was plenty of houses to BUILD.

CONNI: He made everything at the mill: nail, glass, plaster. Only thing he didn't make was the trees for the wood. He *worked* for a living. And what's he get for it? The asthma. Cyrus Eaton's nothing but a grown man in white shoes and short pants walking around town with airs. His mother probably spoiled him, just like your mother spoiled you.

JAMIE is hurt. She catches it right away.

Aw, I'm sorry.

JAMIE: That's all right.

CONNI: How is she? Down there in Kentville?

JAMIE: Went to see her last week. Had to talk to her through a window.

CONNI: She'll be home soon.

JAMIE: Could be a year.

CONNI: A whole year?

JAMIE: What Dr. Gass says. That's the way it is with the TB.

CONNI: And your dad?

JAMIE: Fishing lobster.

CONNI: When'll he be back?

JAMIE: When he's done.

CONNI: Who's takin' care of you?

JAMIE: Auntie Jo comes mornings and overnight. Makes sure I eat during the day and don't die during the night.

CONNI: Hm.

> *JAMIE kicks the dirt, bored. He whistles or sings a Hank Snow song. Perhaps the fireman verse from "I'm Moving On."*

JAMIE: Nothing to do now Gathering of the Clans and Dominion Day is done. One day a year. One day. Ferris wheel, highland dancing, pies, cakes, hot dogs . . . And then nothing.

> *Silence, then:*

FIRE!

CONNI: JAMIE!

JAMIE: Someday, I'm gonna be a reporter! I'm gonna report for the *Amherst Daily News* on all the goings on in Cumberland County.

CONNI: With Cy Eaton bringing the world to Pugwash, you'll have your hands full.

JAMIE: Problem is I got a big voice but a young body. It takes a lot for a boy my age to be heard.

CONNI: Oh, I heard you all the way from Pineo Lodge.

JAMIE: What YOU wanna be, Conni? When you grow up?

CONNI: I dunno. Something not here. Something far away from Pugwash.

JAMIE: Why would anyone wanna leave Pugwash? You got everything: fishing, swimming, farming . . . fishing . . .

CONNI: Ya see? You said it yourself, Jamie. One day a year and then nothing. Me, I'm getting out.

JAMIE: And do what?

CONNI: Something important.

JAMIE: Like what? Be a waitress?

CONNI: What?

JAMIE: You don't need to leave to do that! You could work at Mini's Lunch. Or be a telephone operator like Maggie Chapman.

CONNI: NO! I don't wanna be a waitress, or a telephone operator, or one of those French RC girls canning lobster, come home smellin' of fish. I wanna do something REALLY important. I got . . . ideas, in my head, you know? And I've got an imagination. Maybe I'll go away and study something.

JAMIE: You should talk to some of these Thinkers comin' to town.

CONNI: They're not going to talk to me!

JAMIE: Why not?

CONNI: First off, I'm a girl, and second . . .

JAMIE: What.

CONNI: I'm scared.

JAMIE: Of what?

CONNI: Russians, for one.

JAMIE: *(duh)* They're called Soviets now, Conni.

CONNI: I have this nightmare. I'm on the beach, and there's a submarine coming right up to me. And out jumps a Russian.

He's fat and tall and has big eyebrows like a mean old owl, and he's talking Russian at me. And my legs don't work. I can't get away. And then I wake up screamin'.

JAMIE: How can you be so afraid and so smart at the same time, Conni McPhee?

CONNI: The Russians may have the bomb, Jamie. Know what that means? They could blow us up any time they want. No amount of smarts is going to save you from the bomb. My daddy's ordering a shelter from Debert.

JAMIE: A what?

CONNI pulls out a piece of paper from her back pocket.

CONNI: "Bomb shelters. Ready to order. Be prepared!"

JAMIE: You don't need one of them. Miss Alison showed us how to duck and cover. Besides, who's gonna drop a bomb on Pugwash?

CONNI: All those Thinkers being here? Perfect time to drop a bomb. Like the US did on Hiroshima.

JAMIE spits.

JAMIE: Japs. Had it comin'.

CONNI: *(come now)* Jamie!

JAMIE: Those Japs took my uncle John and put him in a camp and did awful things to him. Auntie Jo told me so. I see a Jap here, I'm gonna kick 'im in the shins.

CONNI: Seems like there's always a war happening somewhere in the world.

JAMIE: Dunno. Just hope it doesn't rain. Otherwise those Thinkers gonna be up to their knees in mud.

A horn.

Ship's in the harbour!

And then a train whistle.

AND the train! What a day! Come on, Conni!

CONNI: What about my daddy's lunch!

JAMIE: Come on! The worlds comin' to Pugwash!

* * *

CONNI: At the train station on Durham Street.
Cy Eaton walking through the white train smoke like Moses.
His homburg in his polished hands.
His blue blazer bright as the sky.
His white shoes like seagulls peeking out of the hem of his pants.
And the press. Like gulls looking for scraps:

BROWN and CY, and perhaps others with flashbulb cameras.

BROWN: Mr. Eaton! Mr. Eaton!

JAMIE: Look at all these people, Conni!

CY: Welcome to Pugwash.

CONNI: Shh now!

BROWN: Mr. Eaton! What's the idea bringing these Thinkers together?

CY: Last year, I read with great interest Lord Russell's manifesto signed by the late Professor Einstein. As Russell wrote, "We must remember our humanity."

CY poses for a snapshot.

Now I'm no scientist. I'm just a humble man from Nova Scotia.

CONNI: Pf.

CY: But what I know is this. The first job of a man is to earn a living. His second job is to think. It is crucial that men of different ideologies and nations exchange their views on nuclear war. The survival of mankind is at stake.

CONNI: See? We're all gonna die.

JAMIE: Sh.

CY: And so I stepped forward with my offer of hosting such a conference.

BROWN: How come the press isn't invited to the meetings, Mr. Eaton? Don't you think the world ought to know what these men are thinking about?

JAMIE: *(shouts)* Yeah, how come we can't go to the meetings!

CONNI: Jamie!

CY: Is that young Jamie Gillis?

JAMIE: And Conni McPhee!

CONNI: *(mortified)* Jamie!

CY: Come on up here, both of you.

They do. CY is kind to them and holds JAMIE forward in front of him.

Look here, everyone. Here's our next generation of Thinkers. What do you want to be when you're older, Jamie?

JAMIE: A REPORTER!

CY: Well then, take this down for your paper, Jamie. And all you men of the press too. These scientists are here representing themselves and not their governments. They need privacy to say what they really think.

BROWN: Where will the scientists be staying, Mr. Eaton?

CY: Some will stay at the lodge, some at the Tide's Inn, and some will stay in these railcars I've had brought in from Ohio. But most will be billeted with the good people of Pugwash, who have agreed to open their homes to our guests. Jamie, would you like to have a Thinker staying with you?

JAMIE: YEAH!

CY: What about you, Conni McPhee?

> *She shakes her head and hides.* CY *laughs and gives* JAMIE *a candy and whispers in his ear.*

JAMIE: Really? WOW!

CY: *(laughs)* No matter what, we'll give people a taste of Nova Scotia hospitality. Welcome to Pugwash!

* * *

> CY *leaves with all the reporters in tow except* BROWN.

CONNI: What'd you do that for?! I don't like getting up in front of people!

JAMIE: We got a Thinker staying with us, Conni! And guess what? He's a SOVIET!

CONNI: Good luck. Before you know, you'll be turning commie red.

JAMIE: *(boloney)* Ahhh!

CONNI: I gotta make sure Daddy got his lunch.

JAMIE: Wait for me!

BROWN: Hey, kid. Hold up a minute.

> *CONNI steps out, but lingers in the shadows to watch the memory. JAMIE comes back. BROWN lights a smoke.*

What's your name again?

JAMIE: Jamie Gillis, sir.

BROWN: I'm Brown. From the *National Review.*

JAMIE: I have not heard of that.

BROWN: No? Heard of *Life Magazine*?

JAMIE: Sure!

BROWN: We're kinda like that. I'm up from New York.

JAMIE: New York!

BROWN: Ever been?

JAMIE: I never been to Halifax!

BROWN: Well then—

JAMIE: Is it true that the Great Fire of 1835 destroyed seventeen city blocks of Manhattan?

BROWN: I actually don't—

JAMIE: That's what I read at school in the *Funk & Wagnalls*.

BROWN: Then it must be true. So you wanna be a reporter, huh?

JAMIE: That is my dream, sir, yes.

BROWN: Well, whatdya say you do some reporting for me?

JAMIE: Really?

BROWN: Sure. You find out things for me. The first job of reporting is gathering information.

JAMIE: I should check with my father, but he's out fishing lobster right now.

BROWN: This conference is only a coupla days, and I've got deadlines.

JAMIE: I already have a job with the *Amherst Daily News*.

BROWN: What'd they pay you?

JAMIE: A quarter a week.

BROWN: I'll pay you a dollar every time you get me the information I need.

JAMIE: *(wow)* A dollar! What kind of information?

BROWN: Reporters aren't allowed to talk to the Thinkers until the press conference near the end, see. So that means we're gonna have to get our stories another way. You get me?

JAMIE: I think so.

BROWN: Now, you've got a Thinker staying with you. A Soviet, did I hear that right?

JAMIE: That's what Mr. Eaton told me.

BROWN: Good. Here's what I want you to do. You talk to that Soviet and then meet me tomorrow morning. Got it?

JAMIE: Done.

> *BROWN extends his hand. JAMIE shakes it.*

BROWN: So, tell me, these street signs in Pugwash. What language are they in?

JAMIE: That's Gaelic, for when we have the Gathering of the Clans.

> *BROWN takes a note.*

BROWN: *(wryly)* Really now. Coulda sworn they were in Russian . . .

* * *

CY: Professor Ogawa.

OGAWA: Mr. Eaton. A great pleasure to meet you.

CY: Your English is excellent, Professor.

OGAWA: I learn from my uncle.

CY: What's that? I'm a little hard of hearing, Professor.

OGAWA: I learn from my uncle. He study in San Francisco. Before the war.

CY: Drink? Sake?

CY has a glass in his hand.

OGAWA: No, thank you for asking.

CY: I don't drink alcohol either. Should have bought up Canada Dry when I had the chance.

CY laughs. OGAWA looks out at the sea:

OGAWA: This is very beautiful place, Mr. Eaton.

CY: Thank you. Bought the place in '28 after two fires destroyed some buildings down by the water. Donated it to the province. Wanted to make sure no one person got that beautiful sunset over the Strait. Look at that! Like a big ball of flame. Have you ever seen such a beautiful thing?

OGAWA: Hm.

ALEX approaches. He coughs.

CY: Ah! Professor Ogawa, allow me to introduce you to Academician Topchiev.

ALEX nods.

Professor Topchiev is Secretary General of the Soviet Academy of Sciences and is leading the Soviet delegation.

OGAWA bows.

Professor Ogawa is here with Yukawa and Tomonaga. If I'm not mistaken, Professor, you are the only one here who witnessed the Hiroshima blast, is that correct?

OGAWA: It seems so, Mr. Eaton.

CY: Well then, I am sure you'll have some . . . insights into this whole business of testing.

(to someone off) Dr. Rotblat, a word, please.

(to the men) I'll let you gentlemen talk. You share the language of science, if no other.

An awkward silence.

ALEX: *(in Russian)* You speak Russian?

OGAWA shakes his head no.

OGAWA: *(in Japanese)* Japanese?

ALEX shakes his head.

(in French) Do you speak French?

ALEX signs: a bit, but it's bad.

English.

ALEX indicates a bit better.

ALEX: Better than French.

An awkwardness.

You speak? Here?

OGAWA: Yes.

ALEX: About?

OGAWA: Strontium-90.

ALEX: Ah.

OGAWA: Testing.

ALEX: Yes.

OGAWA: Impact.

ALEX: Mm.

OGAWA: You? Give lecture? Talk?

ALEX: Ah. Da. Yes.

OGAWA: About?

ALEX struggles for the words.

ALEX: What, we, scientists, must do, to make world . . . safe.

OGAWA: Ah.

Another pause. ALEX makes an effort.

ALEX: Soviet Union and Japan. We agree to end war.

OGAWA: You mean . . . ?

ALEX: How you say . . .

ALEX mimes writing signatures.

OGAWA: Ah. *(a sore point)* You mean the Joint Declaration.

ALEX: Da. We, Soviet Union, we support Japan for United Nations.

OGAWA: Hm.

ALEX: We say Japan not need to pay for cost of war.

OGAWA: Ha.

ALEX: We friends. Now.

OGAWA: But the Islands.

ALEX: *(confused, in Russian)* Huh?

OGAWA: The Kurils. The Islands.

ALEX gets it now.

ALEX: Kurils. Yes. Problem for . . .

OGAWA: Problem?

ALEX: We not agree, uh, we not have understanding on . . . ?

OGAWA: We not agree on Kurils.

The two overlap as needed:

ALEX: No, we . . .

OGAWA: Islands belong to Japan.

ALEX: I-I not mean . . .

OGAWA: They belong to Japan. For thousands of years.

ALEX: What I mean is . . .

OGAWA: Russia steal islands from Japan!

ALEX: No, no, I mean . . .

OGAWA: Russia should not forget Treaty of Portsmouth. Japan defeat Russia.

ALEX doesn't mean what it sounds like:

ALEX: NO!

CY: Everything all right here?

An awkward silence.

OGAWA: Academician Topchiev and I agree that we speak at conference only of science. Nothing else. Yes?

ALEX: . . . Yes.

OGAWA bows and leaves.

ALEX sighs.

CY: . . . Vodka?

ALEX: Vodka. Yes. Please.

* * *

The post office steps. Newspaper bundles. CONNI *has a large book open in front of her and a box of raisins.* JAMIE *has a fishing basket.*

JAMIE: Whatcha doin', Conni McPhee?

CONNI: Waiting for Daddy.

JAMIE: You colouring another cat?

CONNI: Nope.

JAMIE: What then?

CONNI: Not telling.

JAMIE: Come on!

She relents.

CONNI: See this? This is an atlas.

JAMIE: Did you steal that from the school library?

CONNI: I did no such thing! My daddy ordered one last year.

JAMIE: What's with the raisins?

CONNI: I'm licking each raisin and sticking it on every country where there's a Thinker from. See?

JAMIE: Where's Russia?

CONNI: There. That's Moscow, where I'm guessing all three of the Russian scientists live.

JAMIE: Soviets.

CONNI: And here's one for Poland, one for France, one for China, one for Austria, and one for Australia. Seven from all over the States: Chicago and Boston and Ohio and New York. Two from England, three from Japan, and lastly . . .

She licks and places the last two raisins down.

Two from Canada. Hamilton and Victoria.

They stare at it.

JAMIE: Wow. Look how far some of these Thinkers've come. All the way to Pugwash. The new centre of the world!

* * *

ALEX is on the stoop.

He hums/sings a Russian song. Perhaps "Heart, You Have No Rest" or "Amur Waves."

He holds a cigarette in his hands.

His hands absently look for a match in his many pockets. He never looks down, only out at the sea.

He can't find a match.

JAMIE runs on.

He has a homemade fishing rod and a small, worn basket.

JAMIE: Auntie Jo! Auntie Jo!

He stops, seeing ALEX. Doesn't miss a beat.

You won't believe it. I decide to go fishing down at Crescent Beach. I grab a piece of wood from an old six-header trap for a rod. Find a pop bottle, trade it in for a penny, and use it to buy a hook and string from the co-op. Then I find a worm under a rock for bait. And guess what? First cast with that rod, hook and string and . . . Bingo!

He shows the fish, still jumping.

ALEX: Ah! Fish!

JAMIE: Not just any fish! A striped bass!

JAMIE smashes the fish's head against the stoop—just once. It's stunned.

You like fish? Cuz Auntie Jo fries it in butter and it's real tasty.

ALEX: Fish, good!

JAMIE: So you must be the Thinker staying with us!

ALEX: ?

JAMIE: You. Thin-ker.

ALEX: Me? Alexander. Alex.

He holds out his hand. JAMIE *shakes it like he thinks an adult should.*

JAMIE: Jamie Gillis.

ALEX: Ja-mie.

JAMIE: Aren't you hot in that suit, Mr. Alex?

ALEX: Huh?

JAMIE: I say, aren't ya hot?

ALEX: Ah, yes, hot!

ALEX *takes off his jacket, lays it across his thighs.*

JAMIE: So, you're staying with us. Stay. Sleep?

ALEX: Ah yes, sleep. Eat. Think. Write.

JAMIE: Right.

ALEX: Uh, Jamie, you have . . .

JAMIE: A match?

ALEX: Yes!

JAMIE: Sure thing.

JAMIE goes inside.

ALEX checks out the fish. JAMIE returns.

Here ya go. Auntie Jo keeps them on top of the icebox. Habit. From when I was a kid. Don't want a kid messing with matches.

JAMIE lights one.

There is a bit of magic in it for him.

He lights ALEX's cigarette. He feels very adult.

He stares at the flame. Then blows it out and stamps it on the ground.

Never be too careful round here with fire, Mr. Alex. Pugwash has seen six major fires and it is important we don't have another. Do you know the history of the fires of Pugwash, Mr. Alex?

ALEX: Fires? No.

JAMIE: Well. Let me tell you. 1869, 1890, 1898, 1901, 1928, 1929. 1928 being the worst, when not one but two fires wreaked havoc on the town.

As ALEX sits to smoke, JAMIE stands on the top step like it's a stage.

June 29 of that year. Fire breaks out at H.F. Elliot's smoke fish factory, the fire leaping to engulf J.C. Benoit's ice cream parlour, destroyed Dan Sarson's meat market, Orland Thompson's electrical store, the shoe parlor, Alex Peer's restaurant, the Murray block, Charles Woodlock's ice cream, and the well-known Empress Hotel. The blaze then leaps across the street to take Mrs. Ashe's store, the Odd Fellow's Hall, and the home of Silver Allen. The hungry flames then make their way to Crescent Beach, where two cottages are saved, including Pineo Lodge, owned by Cyrus Eaton.

ALEX: Mr. Eaton!

JAMIE: Nevertheless, plans to celebrate Dominion Day two days hence continued! The people of Pugwash will not be put down, Mr. Alex. They will not.

ALEX smokes. He doesn't understand a word, but loves the performance.

August 11 the same year. Within minutes, sheets of flame engulf the house of Mrs. Van Buskirk, and she is trapped. Seeing her predicament, firefighters smash through a window, fight their way through the smoke-filled room, and pass Mrs. Van Buskirk into the fresh air. Alive! But with a bad back.

Meanwhile, Mrs. Frances Schofield watches as her stately home falls victim to the inferno. Sailors from the SS *Freden*, coming up from the harbour, crawl onto her steep roof to wet down the cascade of flying embers. The sailors then go about saving the Baptist church. It is there, with only the bucket brigade to face the raging blaze, that they take a stand. The edifice of the Baptist church is saved!

ALEX: Ah!

JAMIE: But not so the others.

ALEX: Ah.

JAMIE: Leaping and twisting, the flames reach out to envelop the church of England and it is destroyed. Flames leap a quarter mile to consume the property of the Roman Catholic church, where the Reverend Father Macdonald leads a gallant fight. His glebe house is saved! But not so the priest's prized 1926 Chevrolet coupe. Finally, the flames take the canning factory two hundred yards away. It's as if the devil himself battled God in Pugwash that night and won. Confronted with the terrible toll, Mrs. Van Buskirk said it best: "Well. It might have been worse."

ALEX: Hm.

JAMIE: "It might. Have. Been. Worse." Disaster, swift and terrible, has overtaken our little town. But the people of Pugwash carry on! Now, the most important fire took place in 1869—

AUNTIE JO: *(off)* Jamie, did you take my matches?

JAMIE: . . . Maybe. I'm out here with the Thinker.

AUNTIE JO: *(off)* You don't bother that man, now! Leave him be to think.

JAMIE: You're a Soviet, is that correct?

ALEX: Soviet. Me. Da.

JAMIE: My friend Conni, she says you're set to drop the atomic bomb on Pugwash.

ALEX: Huh?

JAMIE demonstrates the A-bomb.

Bomb? Pugwash?

ALEX laughs.

Nyet!

JAMIE: Because the last thing Pugwash needs is more disaster. Do you know Mr. Eaton, Mr. Alex?

ALEX: Mr. Eaton, friend. Da. He is a good man.

JAMIE: That's good to know. That he's your friend. I'll pass that on to . . . people who are interested.

AUNTIE JO: *(off)* Jamie! I'm here to make sure you eat during the day and don't die during the night!

JAMIE: Coming! Mr. Alex? Would you like some fresh striped bass direct from the waters of the Northumberland Strait? Cuz I'll get Auntie Jo started on that for you. And it's best fresh.

ALEX nods and smiles.

ALEX: Fish. Yes.

JAMIE smiles. ALEX goes in. And JAMIE fingers an imaginary dollar.

* * *

CONNI is at the post office. She has her pencil set. Maybe she hums "Love Letters in the Sand" by Pat Boone.

OGAWA passes by. He is looking down, deep in thought.

CONNI sees him. She wants to say something but doesn't.

OGAWA looks up. He's lost his bearings.

He sees CONNI.

OGAWA: Excuse me.

CONNI looks up.

CONNI: Me?

OGAWA: Yes. Can you please tell me: which way is the Masonic Hall?

CONNI: The Mason's? Uh, walk up Water Street here, then make a left on Victoria Street.

OGAWA: Victoria Street.

CONNI: That's right. Then it will be on your right.

OGAWA: Thank you.

He smiles. He starts to leave, but CONNI *bucks up her courage.*

CONNI: Excuse me . . .

OGAWA *stops.*

OGAWA: Yes?

CONNI: Are you a Thinker?

OGAWA *stares at her.*

You're a Thinker, aren't you.

OGAWA *checks his watch. He's got time. He comes closer.*

OGAWA: I am a scientist.

CONNI: You speak English.

OGAWA: I do. Not as well as you, but . . .

CONNI: Sounds pretty good to me.

OGAWA: Thank you. Maybe I practise. With you.

CONNI: Really? *(tickled)* Okay!

He approaches gently.

He bows.

She is mesmerized.

OGAWA: My name is Ogawa.

CONNI: My name is Conni McPhee.

OGAWA: Hello, Conni. May I?

CONNI: Sure!

He sits on the post office steps. She makes room.

You're an Oriental, right?

OGAWA: I am from Japan, yes.

CONNI: I'm sorry.

OGAWA: ??

CONNI: About the bomb. That was terrible what happened.

OGAWA is taken aback by this.

OGAWA: Thank you. How old you are, Conni?

CONNI: Thirteen.

OGAWA: Ah.

CONNI: How old are you, Mr. Ogawa?

OGAWA: Forty-one.

CONNI: My daddy's forty-two, but he doesn't look nothing like you.

OGAWA: No?

CONNI: No. He's got the asthma.

OGAWA: ??

CONNI demonstrates.

Ah.

A silence.

What you drawing, Conni?

CONNI: A cat.

OGAWA: Very nice! Your cat?

CONNI: No, can't have a cat. Cuz of Daddy's asthma. I mean, except for all the barn cats that wander Pugwash living wherever they want. One day I'd like my own cat, that lives just in my room.

OGAWA: My sister had cat.

CONNI: Your sister? Has a cat?

He hesitates. Then:

OGAWA: *(yes)* Hm.

CONNI: Where is she? Is she in Japan?

OGAWA: . . . Yes. She in Japan. And she have cat. Grey cat! Green eyes!

He imitates the cat. CONNI laughs.

CONNI: What's your sister's cat's name.

OGAWA: Uh.

OGAWA doesn't know.

Cat! She call the cat, Cat.

CONNI laughs.

CONNI: You don't know! What's your sister's name?

OGAWA: My sister . . . called Hinata.

CONNI: Hin . . .

OGAWA: Hinata

CONNI: Hinata.

OGAWA: Very good.

CONNI: Can I call my cat that? Hinata?

OGAWA is hesitant.

No?

OGAWA: I . . .

CONNI: That's okay, I'll call it something else.

OGAWA: No, that is good. You call your cat Hinata. My sister like that.

A pause.

CONNI: What're you all doing over there?

OGAWA: You mean . . . ?

CONNI: You Thinkers. Are you planning on figuring out how to use the bomb? Cuz my daddy's got a shelter he's buying.

She pulls the ad from her back pocket to show OGAWA.

I don't want what happened to you to happen to us, you know? Sorry if that's bad to say, but I'm scared Pugwash will get bombed by the Russians. I have this dream sometimes . . .

I'm on the beach, and before you know, there's a submarine coming right up to me. And out jumps a Soviet and he's screaming Russian at me, and my legs, they're not working, and I can't, I can't—

OGAWA touches her. She snaps out of it.

I'm sorry. I didn't mean . . .

OGAWA: Just a dream. No bomb in Pugwash.

OGAWA wipes his brow with a handkerchief.

Hot. Here. In Pugwash.

CONNI: Supposed to rain tomorrow night. That's what the fishermen say. And they're usually right.

OGAWA: Rain—good.

CONNI: Where are you staying? I know lots of people opened their homes. Course, Daddy doesn't like anything Mr. Eaton does, so we didn't think it right . . .

OGAWA: Tide's Inn.

CONNI: Well that's nice.

OGAWA: I must go. We have meeting.

CONNI: Mr. Ogawa. Wait.

She bows, deadly serious. He is touched by the gesture.

I'd like to know more about Japan. I'm here most mornings, waiting with Daddy's lunch. I'd be happy to help you, with your English.

OGAWA: Arigato. Thank you, Conni.

He leaves.

CONNI: *(to herself)* Arigato.

* * *

BROWN: That it?

JAMIE: That's all he told me.

BROWN: There a pay phone around here?

JAMIE: Only one's here at the station, around back.

BROWN: Thanks, kid.

BROWN hands JAMIE a buck.

JAMIE stares at the dollar in awe.

JAMIE: Anything else, sir?

BROWN: Just keep talking to the Russian. Find out what he knows about Cy Eaton.

CY enters unseen, as does CONNI, separately.

JAMIE: Mr. Eaton?

BROWN: Yeah.

JAMIE: There's nothing you don't know already. Everything he says and does is in every paper in the world.

BROWN: I'm sure there's things people don't know about him.

JAMIE: Like what?

BROWN: That's what a good reporter finds out, kid. My organization pays good money for information.

JAMIE: *(sincerely)* Your magazine, you mean?

BROWN: Yeah.

CY: Mr. Brown, correct?

BROWN: That's right.

CY: See me in my office after lunch.

BROWN: Sure thing, Mr. Eaton.

CY: Run along now, Jamie.

CY leaves.

BROWN: Here.

BROWN takes out a bill.

It's called an advance.

He leaves. CONNI is there.

CONNI: What's that guy talkin' to you about?

JAMIE: I'm a reporter!

CONNI: Are ya now.

JAMIE: *National Review*! Next, I'm gonna take some of my archives over to the house, to show our Soviet guest the history of our town.

CONNI: For Pete's sake, Jamie, no one wants to hear about the disasters of Pugwash, let alone a stranger. Let alone a Soviet. You'll give him ideas. You'll make it seem like it's easy to destroy this place.

JAMIE: You should come by, Conni, and you'll see Soviets are like us. Just quieter.

CONNI: Well, I don't have time, because I am teaching Mr. Ogawa, from Japan, how to improve his English.

JAMIE: Are ya now.

CONNI: And I am going to be learning some Japanese myself before their time here is through.

JAMIE: Good.

JAMIE starts to leave.

That'll help you when you're in one of their prisons.

CONNI: *(calling after)* Or when I become someone important!

* * *

CY: Come in.

BROWN: Thank you, Mr. Eaton. I'm surprised you asked me to come.

CY: Why's that?

BROWN: You've made it clear you don't want your scientists disturbed by the press.

CY: I'm not a scientist. What do you want, Mr. Brown?

BROWN: Like the *Times* and the *Globe* and all the other newspapers, I'm here to get a story.

CY: Are you.

BROWN: The *National Review* is a new magazine.

CY: I know it.

BROWN: You do?

CY: I know Buckley's view. Get to it, I'm a busy man.

BROWN: All right then. Why hold these meetings up in Pugwash?

CY: Speak up a little. I'm old and deaf.

BROWN: Why hold these meeting here rather than in the United States?

CY: It would be impossible to hold them in the United States. The Chinamen would not be permitted to come in and if the Russians got in it would be with very great difficulty.

BROWN: Sounds more like a job for the United Nations.

CY: Who can tell you more about the science of radiation? These men here, or some paper pushers in New York.

BROWN: Mr. Eaton, your large empire of coal, iron ore, and railroads is worth over 1.5 billon dollars. How is it—?

CY: Two billion.

BROWN: I stand corrected. How is it—?

CY: Made a million dollars before I was thirty, and a helluva lot more before I lost it all in the Great Depression, but I've built it back up tenfold.

BROWN: How is it that someone like yourself, on a list of the fifty richest men in America—

CY: Twenty richest.

BROWN: How is it that a capitalist like yourself can support bringing our enemy—

CY: What enemy?

BROWN: These men from Soviet Russia and Red China.

CY: They're scientists, not politicians.

BROWN: But those countries are devoted to communism.

CY: This conference will prove that men of different languages, philosophies, and countries can get together and discuss crucial questions, come to a common understanding, and part great friends.

BROWN: But we're at war with these countries.

CY: The Cold War is doing nothing but creating mindless suspicion.

BROWN: Khrushchev has told Americans, "Your grandchildren will live under socialism." So how can any responsible American government be anything *but* suspicious.

CY: We're giving up our freedoms for hallucinations.

BROWN turns the page of his notebook.

BROWN: Mr. Eaton, is it true that you've been fingerprinted and investigated by the FBI on three occasions?

CY: Of course. Most big American corporations occasionally do some work for the government that is considered classified. Why it's called that I don't know because none of it is really very secret. In the case of a man as old as I am, fingerprinting is quite a humiliation. I've proven myself a loyal and devoted citizen.

BROWN: What's wrong with finding out if that person is *still* a loyal and devoted citizen.

CY: Because. It's propaganda. When I see a nation coming to greatness through the activities of its policemen, I get concerned, Mr. Brown. The FBI and CIA are just some of the scores of agencies in the United States that are engaged in snooping, in informing, in creeping up on people.

BROWN: Alger Hiss, Julius and Ethel Rosenberg—

CY: These are a small percentage of cases. If you had to take the police forces of all the cities and of all the counties and of all the states and all the federal agencies, and add them up, well, Hitler in his time never had such spying as there is in America today.

BROWN: Now wait a second, are you saying—?

CY: Every day there goes out from some department of government boasts of America's greatness, of its power, and what it's going to do to the other fella if he doesn't behave himself. I don't believe we have any right to tell anyone that we'll shoot them to death if they don't accept our view of destiny. I swear, there is more spirit of war in the United States than in any other country in the world.

BROWN: Can I quote you on that?

CY: Nothing I say here is secret. The American government believes communism is a frightful thing that ought to be destroyed, and that any suggestion it be allowed to live is betraying our country. And all of that's nonsense. We can't destroy communism; it's here to stay.

BROWN: But still, isn't it critical to have a massive force that will deter the Russians from wanting to attack us?

CY: The Russian people don't want war. And we don't need any massive nuclear retaliation to keep it that way.

BROWN turns a page.

BROWN: Mr. Eaton, do you consider yourself a "liberal"?

CY: Some people label me that but—

BROWN: Some say "liberal thinking" is a threat to our survival and freedom.

CY: How can we consider ourselves free when, if you want to speak out against the government, you're branded a liberal or a communist or a fellow traveller, or whatever word your people decide to use.

BROWN: What you are doing here may well be illegal. It may well contravene the Logan Act, which, as you know, forbids unauthorized citizens from negotiating with foreign governments.

CY: When J. Edgar Hoover asked Congress to call me in front of the House Un-American Activities Committee, you know what I did? I told Hoover to go to hell.

BROWN: Wealth has its privileges.

CY: Perhaps. But I am an old man. And I'm not afraid of the American government, or poverty, or death, or any right-wing conservative press. The only thing I fear is a nuclear war that will destroy our planet. And I will do everything in my power to make sure that doesn't happen.

BROWN: Even if it means breaking the law?

CY: I'll let the courts decide that.

BROWN: Question. My final one, I promise.

CY relents.

Bertrand Russell, who inspired this conference, when given the choice between a nuclear war and living under Communism, would take Communism. What about Cyrus Eaton?

CY: No one in the world would be more unhappy under Communism than I.

BROWN: But would you rather die than live under it?

CY is silent.

I suggest, Mr. Eaton, that you can't have it both ways.

BROWN is leaving.

CY: I have on good authority that the CIA is paying off some journalist to do their dirty work. To discredit anyone who has anything contrary to say about the current US administration. Operation Mockingbird, they call it. Now, you wouldn't happen to know anything about *that*, would you, Mr. "Brown" of the *National Review*?

BROWN: I'm not the enemy, Mr. Eaton. I love my country just as much as you.

He leaves. CY is uneasy.

* * *

CONNI: We watch the Thinkers wander down Victoria Street to the old Masonic Hall. Different men, from distant parts of the world, speak languages we'd never dreamt of. Russian, Chinese,

Japanese, Hungarian, German, Polish. Not like the sailors in the harbour, cussing and grunting, but some kind of whirlpool of words, like birds on the beach, all chattering about something only they know about.

JAMIE: Look at them all, Conni! Look at all them Thinkers! Can you believe it?

They peer through the windows.

CONNI: We stare through stained glass below the bull's eye over the door. Inside, kitchen chairs collected from all over Pugwash. Tables borrowed from every church, a blackboard from the nursery school. The edges filled with birds and flowers. But in white chalk . . .

JAMIE: What's all those squiggles on the board?

CONNI: Equations.

JAMIE: For what?

CONNI: How would I know? Disaster, no doubt.

CY enters.

CY: Jamie!

JAMIE: Ah!

CONNI: Mr. Eaton!

CY: What're you doing there?

CONNI: We were, we were . . .

JAMIE: I'm a reporter now, Mr. Eaton, so I have to keep a close eye on what's going on.

CY smiles.

CY: Well done, Jamie Gillis.

He gives them both candy.

But this is a private meeting. No one allowed in the Hall unless I say so. Understand?

JAMIE: Yes, sir! Are you friends with the Russians, Mr. Eaton?

CONNI: Jamie!

CY: What's that?

JAMIE: Cuz some people think we should not be talking to people who might drop a bomb on Pugwash.

CONNI: Jamie Gillis!

CY: No, that's all right, Conni. Russian people, Jamie, are just like us. So yes, some Russians, like these men here, I would consider friends.

JAMIE: Can I quote you on that, sir?

CY: Sure thing, Jamie. But be careful who you talk to, ya hear?

CY leaves.

CONNI: I cannot believe you. Hey, where you going!

JAMIE: I just made myself another dollar!

She stays, thinks, then sneaks up to the window and looks inside.

* * *

Inside the Hall. CY speaks. ALEX and OGAWA are there, listening.

CY: Gentlemen. We live in a time of great danger. The Atomic Society has announced we are two minutes to midnight on the Doomsday Clock. It's been just over ten years since the events of Hiroshima and Nagasaki, and we still don't really know the scientific effects of what happened. And if the recent tests of the new hydrogen bomb are any indication, we're moving closer to world war and not away from it.

Before you begin, I'd like to play a recording Lord Russell has sent from London.

CY turns on a reel to reel recorder.

RUSSELL: *(voice-over)* We find ourselves in a situation very like that between Athens and Sparta. After thirty years, each side became exhausted by an escalating war. We must learn to think in a new way. We must ask ourselves: Shall we put an end to the human race? Or shall mankind renounce war forever? Above all, remember your humanity.

He turns off the recorder.

CY: Mr. Rotblat will now take the chair. Good luck, gentlemen.

CY leaves and CONNI runs off.

* * *

BROWN is on the pay phone, smoking.

BROWN: Yeah. I got something. On Eaton. I tell ya it's— Hang on. I gotta drop another dime.

He puts in another dime.

Let me tell you something. It'll be the worth the wait . . .

They've hung up.

. . . Shit.

* * *

CONNI sits on the post office steps drawing.

OGAWA is there with his briefcase.

OGAWA: Konnichiwa!

He bows.

CONNI: Konnichiwa!

She bows.

OGAWA: Very good! Now, Conni, you help me?

CONNI: Sure. With what?

OGAWA: I send letter. To Japan.

CONNI: Okay!

He hands her the envelope.

I'll give it to my daddy. He'll know what to do with it. I figure it's gotta go to Halifax first or maybe Moncton. It may take a while, Mr. Ogawa.

OGAWA: That okay. I want it have Canadian stamp on it.

CONNI: Is this going to your sister?

OGAWA: Oh. No.

CONNI: Can I write to her?

OGAWA: Ah . . .

CONNI: I'd like to tell her I know you, and that I know about her cat, and that I want to name my cat after her.

OGAWA: Conni . . .

CONNI: Just a short note. Not sure how much it would cost, but I'm sure Daddy would take care of it. Please, Mr. Ogawa?

OGAWA: My sister . . . she not understand English.

CONNI: Then teach me to write it in Japanese.

OGAWA: That is very hard, Conni.

CONNI: Please? I'd do anything to write to someone in another country.

OGAWA considers.

OGAWA: Come, you sit here. We write letter.

He reaches into his case and pulls out beautiful writing paper. He pulls out an ink well and a special pen.

CONNI: What's that?

OGAWA: Kanji.

CONNI: Huh?

OGAWA: See?

He writes a symbol in kanji. He shows it to her.

CONNI: Holy moly! Is that really a word?

OGAWA: It means "hello."

CONNI: It's like art, Mr. Ogawa.

OGAWA: Like your pictures.

He continues writing as . . .

* * *

ALEX is on the stoop. He is reading some 8" x 11" pieces of white paper. JAMIE enters with an old newspaper.

JAMIE: This is it, Mr. Alex. This is worth more to me than any comic, or any coin, or any stamp Auntie Jo says I should be collecting. Right here. Look at this.

He shows ALEX. ALEX looks for a light, and JAMIE has the matches ready.

ALEX: Old, yes?

JAMIE: Oh it's old all right.

ALEX: What it say?

JAMIE: The greatest story Pugwash has ever known. The story of *(a goddess)* Mary Crowley.

ALEX: Tell. This story.

JAMIE doesn't need the paper. He's told it a million times.

JAMIE: September 30, 1869. Ten p.m. Mrs. Crowley springs from her bed to find the whole body of the house in flames. With babe in arms, she breaks free from the flames and runs outside. But upstairs three children are still trapped.

The eldest daughter, Mary, but twelve years old, comes to the window. Her mother urges her to throw herself out, but she refuses: *(as Mary)* "No, my other brother and sister must be saved." She returns through the heat and smoke, takes her sleeping brother in her arms, carries him to the window, and springs to the ground.

But does she stop there, Mr. Alex? No! She then RETURNS THROUGH THE FLAMES, climbs the smouldering stairs, grabs her younger sister, and brings her to the window.

With the flames coming up around her, Mary drops the child safely into the arms of her mother. Then Mary herself throws herself ONCE MORE from the window. When her mother comes to her aid, Mary says: "I am done, Mother. But I have saved my brother and sister from being burnt up."

And to this day, she is remembered in the Catholic cemetery here in Pugwash, with a large memorial to mark her sacrifice: "Mary E. Crowley lies beneath this sod, a victim of fraternal love."

She saved her family, Mr. Alex. She was just a kid, but she saved people. Mary's a hero, is she not? Is she not as worthy a hero as those of ancient Rome?

ALEX butts his smoke.

ALEX: She brave, this Mary. You brave?

JAMIE: Me? No. I wouldn't know what to do if there was a real fire. But I'd sure like to report on it.

ALEX: You help me now, Jamie?

JAMIE: Help you?

ALEX nods to the papers.

ALEX: Tomorrow. I must read. To others. You help me. With English.

JAMIE: Sure. If I can.

ALEX: Secretary. She translate Russian to English. I want to speak.

JAMIE: Okay.

ALEX has memorized it with some difficulty.

ALEX: "Good morning, my fellow scientists." Is a-a—

JAMIE: It is a pleasure.

ALEX: "It is a pleasure to be here today at this . . . "

JAMIE: Important.

ALEX: "Important meeting."

ALEX tries again.

"Good morning, my fellow scientists. It is a pleasure to be here today at this important meeting. I speak today on the re . . . "

JAMIE: Responsibility . . .

ALEX: Res—

JAMIE: Responsibility.

ALEX: "Responsibility of scientist."

JAMIE: Very good, Mr. Alex.

Both scenes come together:

CONNI: Read it to me now, please?

OGAWA: *(reading)* "My name is Conni. I am thirteen years old. I live in Canada. I drew a cat. Guess what I named it? Hinata! One day, I hope to be someone important. Sincerely yours."

Now, I teach you your name in kanji.

OGAWA holds her hand as she draws the characters.

JAMIE: Shall we go on, Mr. Alex?

ALEX: We go in now. Eat. Drink. Read more later.

ALEX goes in. JAMIE picks up ALEX's papers and stares at them.

OGAWA: I must go now. Late. You mail these, Conni, okay?

CONNI picks up the letter and looks at her handiwork.

ALEX: *(calling)* Jamie!

JAMIE runs inside. CONNI stares at her paper.

CONNI: "Conni."

End of Act One.

ACT TWO

ALEX: Good morning, fellow scientists. Please forgive my speaking. I learn more English in two days in Pugwash than in fifty years in Moscow.

CY chuckles. ALEX reads:

It gives me great pleasure to speak to you on responsibility of scientist.

I and my fellow Soviets, Kuzin and Skobeltsyn, we agree that science misused by nations for competitive interests as world powers is not good. It make possible the destruction of mankind. Science used by all nations for human knowledge and improvement is good. We scientists have responsibility for constructive use of science.

(in Russian) Thank you.

CY: Questions. Professor Ogawa?

OGAWA: Will you tell Moscow what you discover here?

ALEX: We will report to Moscow, yes. But now, we say this here, in Pugwash.

CY: Mr. Rabinowitch?

OGAWA is not done.

OGAWA: Will USSR stop testing RDS bomb in Kazakhstan?

ALEX: Professor Ogawa. We tell our leaders what we know, then they do what they do.

OGAWA: Will you, Academician Topchiev, sign agreement on non-testing.

ALEX: We must first—

OGAWA: Will American stop testing at Nevada? Will England stop testing at Christmas Island? We must stop testing.

CY: Dr. Powell, then Professor Doty, then Mr. Thirring.

OGAWA: Do we all agree here that we must tell public and governments to stop testing until we know more?

ALEX: Please, Professor Ogawa.

CY: Professor Ogawa, one at a time, please.

OGAWA: This is what responsibility means, does it not, Academician? That science must prevail over politics? That we speak the truth?

* * *

BROWN: The responsibility of the scientist, huh.

JAMIE: That's what he talked about today.

BROWN: Where're the notes?

JAMIE: He needed them for the talk. But I bet I could get them tonight when he isn't looking.

BROWN lights a smoke.

BROWN: I want you to sneak into the Mason's Hall.

JAMIE: What? But that's not allowed.

BROWN: You wanna be a reporter, don'tcha?

JAMIE: Sure, but . . .

BROWN: Well then? Reporters sometimes need to do things that they're not supposed to do. That's how you get the real scoop. Being in dangerous places.

JAMIE: Why don't *you* sneak in?

BROWN: They'd see me right away. But they'd never suspect you. Heck, they'd never even notice you were there.

JAMIE hesitates.

I'll give you a byline. Know what that means?

JAMIE: Uh uh.

BROWN: Means when I write this article, I'm gonna say it's "by" me AND Jamie Gillis. Now that's a real professional credit. You got a byline, people'll take you seriously.

JAMIE: But Mr. Eaton told me . . .

BROWN: I'm going to level with you, Jamie. Mr. Eaton is a bad man.

JAMIE: He is not! He's a Nova Scotian!

BROWN: All right, but he still lives and works in Cleveland, which is in America. And he is a communist sympathizer. And talking to Reds in America is against the law. Now if we don't do our job, as reporters, he could put you, and your little town here, and everyone in North America, at risk of a nuclear attack.

JAMIE: But he, he's been real nice to me . . .

BROWN: Sure he has. It's what they do, the Reds. They pretend they're your friend, and then BAM.

JAMIE is still hesitant.

Now: you sneak into that Hall tomorrow . . .

BROWN holds out the bills.

Lightning. CONNI *grabs* OGAWA *by the leg.*

Sorry! Don't like lightning. Don't like the thunder that comes later.

OGAWA: I teach you something, Conni. Something I do with my sister. When she your age, she also scared of lightning. So, when the lightning come, we count.

Lightning.

One, two . . .

TOGETHER: . . . three, four, five, six . . .

Thunder, nearer.

OGAWA: See? Every time we count, the less and less numbers, that mean the thunder—

It comes closer again.

CONNI: How's that supposed to make me feel better.

OGAWA: When you count, you know. No surprise. Thunder, lightning, it is all science. It is all knowable.

They watch the rain. Then:

CONNI: My friend Jamie, he says that Japan deserved the bomb. He says that you people did terrible things during the war. He says that the US dropped the bomb to end the war faster. Is that true?

OGAWA considers.

OGAWA: Conni, I tell you a story, okay?

CONNI: Sure.

OGAWA: Long time ago. There is a man. He famous mathematician. His name is Archimedes.

CONNI: Archimedes.

OGAWA: He build fantastic inventions. He even help build weapons for his country. But he is good man. He only want to think, solve problems, that all.

CONNI: Okay . . .

OGAWA: Archimedes is on beach. He is writing formula in sand, with stick, solving big problem. But just then. Soldier come. He draw a sword. He say, "Come with us." Archimedes say, "Wait, I am solving problem!" Soldier say, "No." And he wipe his formula from sand. And then he kill Archimedes.

CONNI: What?

OGAWA: Soldier scared of Thinker. Soldier want to control Thinker. Soldier use Thinker. To end war earlier. You think that is right?

CONNI: No.

OGAWA: Me neither.

Lightning. This time CONNI *starts the count . . .*

CONNI: One, two, three . . .

Thunder. She doesn't flinch. OGAWA *smiles.*

* * *

Thunder. JAMIE *sits on the porch, under cover.*

ALEX *runs up, his coat over his head.*

JAMIE: You made it!

ALEX: Yes. Rain!

JAMIE: Ya know what they say in Pugwash: if you want the weather to change, wait a minute.

ALEX *takes out a cigarette and* JAMIE *lights it. It's become a ritual.*

JAMIE *sits, while* ALEX *stands.*

They both stare out at the ocean.

See out there. On a clear day you can see PEI. They say if there's clouds over there, that means bad weather here. That's what my father told me.

Lightning.

Lots of boats gone down out there. They say on some nights you can see the ghost ship of the Northumberland Strait sailing toward the horizon, its three masts on fire. And a bell, tolling. Some sailors been known to make for the ship, thinking they could rescue all those aboard, but when they get closer, it's vanished. Scary that something could, ya know . . . vanish.

Some days I worry. When my father's out there. Never know what can happen.

ALEX listens to him. He reaches out his hand to touch JAMIE's head, but doesn't.

Lightning.

Do you have a family, Mr. Alex?

ALEX: ??

JAMIE: Children? Like me?

ALEX: Ah yes, boy. Like you. But . . .

ALEX looks down.

JAMIE: What's his name?

ALEX: His name Kostya.

JAMIE: Kost . . .

ALEX: James. Jamie. Konstantin. Kostya.

JAMIE: "Kostya." What's he like?

ALEX: He . . . like you. He like talking.

JAMIE: That's me!

Thunder.

Mr. Alex. Whose side is everyone on?

ALEX: ??

JAMIE: Like when I play cops and robbers, I know whose side I'm on. I'm either a cop or a robber. And cops are good and robbers are . . . not as good. But with the Soviets and Red China and everything, I get confused.

ALEX: Me also.

JAMIE: Do you? Who are the cops and who are the robbers?

ALEX: During World War Two, Americans and USSR work together. Now? We enemies. Before, Japan and Russia enemies. But now, we try to be friends.

JAMIE: That's what I mean. What happened?

ALEX takes out a small weathered photo. He hands it to JAMIE.

Who's this?

ALEX: That Kostya. As a boy.

JAMIE: How old is he now?

ALEX: Kostya, he . . . die.

JAMIE: Your son died?

ALEX: Yes.

JAMIE: But . . . How?

ALEX: Kostya fly plane. Pilot. He fight for Soviet Union in Korea. You know war in Korea?

JAMIE: I think so.

ALEX: He shot down. He die.

JAMIE: Oh no.

ALEX stares at the photo.

ALEX: Nineteen. He still a boy.

JAMIE: I'm sorry to hear that, Mr. Alex.

ALEX: When that happen, my thinking, it change.

JAMIE: Whatdya mean?

ALEX: No child deserve to die. No matter where they are from, no matter if they child of cop or robber. War, no matter what kind it is, it mean children die. You see?

Thunder. It's loud. JAMIE *flinches. And now* ALEX *puts an arm around him.*

You no worry, Jamie. Your father—he come home soon.

* * *

Thunder continues. The storm is brewing.

The Masonic Hall.

CONNI: What are you doing here?

JAMIE: *(caught)* Nothin.' What are you doing here?

CONNI: *(caught)* Nothin'. Mr. Ogawa from Japan is speaking at the conference today, and it being the last day, I wanted to see him . . . go in.

JAMIE: Well all right then.

CONNI: Where you going?

JAMIE: Be quiet, will ya.

CONNI: Jamie! You can't go in there.

JAMIE: I'll explain later. Here they come. Just don't say anything!

He sneaks in under a table or some such thing.

* * *

Thunder.

CONNI: They walk into the Hall. They're as serious as storm clouds. The air thick and heavy like an approaching gale. This is the moment. This is their last chance.

CONNI watches through the window as before.

* * *

Thunder. The lights flicker.

CY: Gentlemen, your last session is on testing and the controls for nuclear weaponry. Mr. Ogawa will begin on the effects of radiation.

OGAWA: Arigato, Mr. Eaton, and thank you again for hosting this very important conference.

We now know an atom bomb can be made twenty-five hundred times as powerful as the one that destroy small cities of Hiroshima and Nagasaki. But one hydrogen bomb could destroy a big city like London, New York, Moscow. In the course of a few centuries, these cities recover. If many H-bombs are used there will be universal death. But sudden only for a minority. For the majority, a slow torture of disease.

Why? Because we now know, since the Bikini Atoll test, that nuclear bombs can spread destruction over a much wider area and for longer time.

Strontium-90 is the radioactive isotope produced by nuclear fission. A bomb, no matter on land or under water, send Strontium-90 into the upper air. These radioactive particles reach surface of earth. Dark dust, black rain. That is what infect Japanese fishermen and fish.

In Hiroshima, one hundred thousand additional cases of radiation poisoning. In a general war, hundreds of millions would be killed outright by the heat blast. Additional hundreds of millions doomed by the delayed effects of radiation.

Thunder.

CY: Thank you, Professor.

OGAWA: I speak now for Tomonaga and Yukawa. Further nuclear testing biggest worry for Japanese. Hiroshima a tragedy. I myself witness it. But anti-Americanism, anti-Soviet feelings—these not as strong as fear of radiation. Thank you.

CY: Questions? Academician Topchiev.

ALEX: But, we, scientists, what we do?

OGAWA: Stop testing.

ALEX: Professor Ogawa . . .

OGAWA: Stop testing.

ALEX: *(a lost cause)* We have not power to . . .

OGAWA: USSR has power. America has power. Japan no longer has power. Stop testing.

CY: Dr. Rotblat, then Dr. Rabinowitch—

ALEX: We need create strategic balance.

OGAWA: And new weapons? What then?

ALEX: We can tell government, but will they listen?

OGAWA: Balance lead to stockpiling.

ALEX: It is not easy . . . to . . .

OGAWA: Will USSR use bomb?

They overlap:

ALEX: I cannot say . . .

OGAWA: You invade Japan, will not sign peace treaty, you take . . .

ALEX: The Kurils belong to Soviet Union.

OGAWA: And will Soviet use bomb on Japan to protect them?

ALEX: Japan work with Hitler. In Russia, millions die. In five years—five years! Millions!

OGAWA: In Japan, one hundred fifty thousand die in one day! ONE DAY!

A huge crack of thunder. The lights flicker.

Then church bells—an alarm. Shouts from outside. CONNI has run off.

ALEX: What is that?

VOICE: *(off)* FIRE!

CY: What in the name of—?

VOICE: *(off)* FIRE!

CONNI runs into the Hall.

CONNI: It's the post office! It's on fire!

The men stand. JAMIE bounds from his place.

JAMIE: The post office?

ALEX holds him back.

ALEX: Jamie! What you doing here?

JAMIE: My archives!

JAMIE runs out. And all follow.

* * *

The bells, people shouting, chaos. OGAWA and ALEX call for their child friends. CY calls out that the post office is on fire. To come quick.

They are all there, watching the flames. Then:

CY: Bucket brigade!

They all form a chain and assist putting out the fire.

CONNI: The smell of smouldering twine, the crackle of old news. And the sky red as an exploding sun. People rushing with buckets of water. And my daddy, my daddy runs in to try and put it out, but the smoke, and his asthma, and he falls down, gasping for breath.

* * *

All are on stage.

CONNI: Daddy! Daddy!

CY: John Deekan, put Conni's dad in my car, then pick up Dr. Gass, and get to the Tatamagouche hospital straight away.

CY follows them out. CONNI turns on JAMIE.

CONNI: *(furious, crying)* You see what you done, Jamie Gillis? Ya see?

JAMIE: Me?! I didn't do anything!

CONNI: If your archives hadn't been here, there wouldn't BE a fire. And now look. I'm gonna lose my daddy. I'm gonna lose my whole LIFE. And all because of YOU. You and your stupid archives! You and your stupid fires! You and your stupid HISTORY! Well I hope your mama DIES in Kentville. I hope she never has to come back to see all the things you've done. I hate you, Jamie Gillis!

CONNI runs off.

BROWN: Hey, kid. You got anything? My boss wants that story about Eaton and the Reds by tomorrow.

JAMIE: Get away from me.

BROWN: Here: here's another coupla bucks—

JAMIE throws the bills he's got at BROWN.

JAMIE: Keep your money! Cuz I wouldn't tell you what happened, not for a hundred dollars!

CY: What's going on here?

JAMIE: He told me you were a traitor, Mr. Eaton.

CY: Is that why you snuck into the Mason's Hall. Because of him?

JAMIE: He gave me money to tell on you and Mr. Alex, and now . . .

JAMIE is overwhelmed with guilt.

. . . now I don't have nothing. No friends, no archives, nothing.

JAMIE runs off. CY grabs BROWN.

CY: Now you listen here. You write your story. You sling as much mud as you want. But don't you ever mess with these kids, ya hear me?

BROWN: And here I thought old Cyrus was a man of peace.

CY: Get outta here.

BROWN: See you in Washington, Mr. Eaton.

BROWN leaves. CY goes in the opposite direction.

ALEX and OGAWA stare at the now smouldering flames.

* * *

JAMIE is on his porch with a box of matches.

He lights one. Stares at it. Angry.

He waits till it burns down, burning his fingers.

He winces. Drops it.

He takes another. Lights it. Waits.

OGAWA walks by. He sees JAMIE burn himself on the second match. He sees him about to light a third and approaches.

OGAWA: You are Jamie, yes?

JAMIE looks up.

You Conni's friend.

JAMIE: Not anymore.

JAMIE turns the matchbox over in his hand.

OGAWA comes closer.

OGAWA: My name is Ogawa. I am—

JAMIE: I know who you are. You're a Jap. People say you're a Thinker, but my uncle says you hurt our Canadian boys real bad in Hong Kong, in those prisons. My uncle says the bomb was a *good* thing. He says you deserved it for all the horrible things you done, and that's what I believe too.

JAMIE lights a match.

OGAWA: What are you doing there?

JAMIE: What's it look like? Gonna burn down all of Pugwash. Stupid town. Never meant nothing to anybody, then people come from away, our chance to shine, and what happens? We got a fire, a fire that . . .

OGAWA comes closer.

So what else is there to do, but burn it all up, burn it all down, cuz this little town isn't gonna mean anything to anyone or the world anyway. It's cursed. It's cursed and better to burn it away than live with . . .

JAMIE gets up, and in a flurry and fury starts lighting match after match. OGAWA drops his case now and runs to stamp out each match, then snatches the box from JAMIE's hands.

JAMIE tries to run, but OGAWA nabs him, firm but not rough.

Let me go, let me go!

JAMIE tries to kick him in the shins, but OGAWA's got hold of him.

OGAWA: Jamie. Jamie!

JAMIE's anger and hatred burns away, and he dissolves into tears.

(gently) Shhhh. Listen to me. Listen.

I am working for university. I am on an island in the bay. We could see it, Hiroshima, across the water. Like you see PEI, you know?

JAMIE nods.

August. Monday. Morning. I am outside, walking to work. I hear a hum. Like a horsefly. I look up. I see an American bomber. Far up. So far . . .

Then a flash. Like the sun. And then I count.
One, two, three, four . . .
Till I am at thirty. And then . . .
Boom. Like thunder.

I look up, a cloud, it move up, big, so big . . .
Like a big whale reaching for the top of the sky.

We take boat. To the city. We get off:
Everything. Gone. On fire. So hot, so very hot.

My sister, she live there. And so I start to run. Through the city, the fire. I run to my sister's house. She is alive, yes. But she badly burned. She have a cat and cat is dead.

She die three weeks later.

And I think: no. This will never happen again. Never.

But three days later: Nagasaki. And I think, no, never a third time. Never a third time there is fire from the sky.

OGAWA reaches down and picks up the box of matches. He hands it to JAMIE.

Jamie. You, me . . . we must stop this.

* * *

CONNI is on the beach. She has been crying. She has her pencil set with her and is drawing.

ALEX walks down the strand.

He sees her. Stops. Then approaches. It bears a resemblance to her nightmare.

ALEX: *(in Russian)* Hello.

CONNI: *(startled)* Ahh!

She scuttles backward, considers running, but is frozen. ALEX stands unknowingly between her and her pencils.

ALEX: *(gently)* Hey, hey! It okay!

He puts up his hands.

I don't hurt you. See?

CONNI: You're a Russian, aren't you?

ALEX: Yes. Me, Soviet Russian.

CONNI: You're the enemy.

ALEX: No, no enemy. Friend.

He approaches, but she backs away.

CONNI: Can I have my pencils, please?

ALEX: *(in Russian)* Huh?

CONNI points.

Ah! Pencil!

He hands her the pencils.

My name Alex. You?

CONNI: Conni.

ALEX: Conni . . .

He smiles. He remembers.

You Jamie's friend, no?

CONNI: Not anymore.

ALEX: No?

CONNI: He told me we can trust you, but I don't believe anything he says. I think you're going to take over the world and make us slaves. That's what my daddy says.

ALEX: . . . Slave? Nyet. Friend!

CONNI: You have the bomb now. You can do whatever you like. Isn't that right?

ALEX takes her in. He points at her drawing.

ALEX: What, what you . . . draw there.

CONNI: None of your business.

ALEX: You are artist, Conni?

CONNI: No, I just have a big imagination.

ALEX: Who is this?

CONNI: That is Mr. Ogawa.

ALEX: Ogawa!

CONNI: This here is Mr. Ogawa, and this is his sister, Hinata, see? And this is the atom bomb going off, and this is his sister's cat. And see here, this is all the fish in the ocean dead from the radioactive stuff that you've been talking about here in Pugwash.

ALEX: Hm.

He sees it in her. He searches for the words.

Conni.
You afraid?

CONNI: Well who wouldn't be, Mr. Alex. All you scientists, you Thinkers, you're just going to kill us with the things you discover.

ALEX: Ah.

He looks around.

He takes up a stick and some rocks.

CONNI: What are you . . . ?

ALEX: Now Alex, he draw something.

Using rocks, seaweed, his stick, perhaps a washed-up bottle, he creates a simple diagram of a chain reaction.

You see this? Neutron. Say.

CONNI: Neutron.

ALEX: Good. Plutonium. Say.

CONNI: Plutonium.

ALEX: Good.

He demonstrates the chain reaction, ending with him pretending to be a bomb.

You understand?

CONNI: The neutron hits the plutonium and then—

ALEX: More and more reactions yes, and then . . .

TOGETHER: Boom!

ALEX: Da. This drawing, Conni, in sand, this formula for nuclear bomb. This is what you fear.

She stares at it.

Now. You.

He hands her the stick.

CONNI: What?

ALEX: Now YOU are scientist, now YOU are Thinker.

CONNI: Me, a Thinker . . . ?

ALEX: Da! And now you must decide.

CONNI: Decide what?

ALEX: What you do with this formula now? What you do with this science. Use it? Kick it away? What you do, Conni? Scientist, Thinker?

She looks at the formula.

CONNI: I'll tell you what I'm gonna do.
I'm gonna let the tide wash it away.
Let the sea do with it what it wants.

ALEX: Ah . . .

CONNI: But I'll tell you one thing, Mr. Alex. I'll never forget it's *here.*

CONNI points to her head.

* * *

CY: Gentlemen, this is the final communiqué of this conference.

And when you consider the political tension and distrust between East and West, a statement that speaks of the responsibility of scientists is a sort of miracle. "This is a decisive epoch of mankind. It is comparable in man's mastery of fire. Unrestricted nuclear war would be a disaster of unprecedented magnitude. And the greatest danger is from the United States and the USSR, who might intervene with nuclear weapons in disputes of smaller states." The overwhelming majority of scientists here signed this document. Congratulations!

* * *

OGAWA comes to ALEX.

OGAWA: Japan. Russia. Long history of conflict. Two wars in fifty years.

ALEX: We make peace, you and I? Maybe not Soviet Union and Japan. But you, me: we make peace. Yes?

ALEX bows. OGAWA is moved.

OGAWA: It is a start.

* * *

CONNI returns to the present. JAMIE is there, getting progressively older, but still the paper boy at heart.

CONNI: Sixty years ago.
On a beach in Pugwash.
I drew my future in the sand.

JAMIE: "1963. Pugwash scientists help broker Partial Test Ban Treaty!"

CONNI: I left. Angry. Moved away.

JAMIE: "1972. Pugwash members assist with Anti-Ballistic Missile Treaty!"

CONNI: And I became a mathematician.

JAMIE: "1981. Pugwash scientists caution governments against nuclear weapons in space!"

CONNI: I joined a movement of scientists who help create treaties, to end testing.

JAMIE: "1989. Pugwash warns of the dangers posed by the breakup of the Soviet Union!"

CONNI: But you never left. You stayed in Pugwash. Became a reporter.

JAMIE: "1995. The Pugwash Conferences and Joseph Rotblat awarded Nobel Peace Prize!"

CONNI: I never spoke to you after that fire. After my daddy died. I held hate for you deep in my heart for so long. And now . . .

JAMIE: 2017. Jamie Gillis passes away peacefully at the age of seventy.

CONNI: I'm heading to Switzerland tomorrow. To be an expert. To be "someone important." A rogue state. A nuclear weapon. And I'm to convince governments, as we've been doing for six decades now, that owning bombs ten times the size of Hiroshima will not lead to peace.

But how can I help make peace in the world when I couldn't even make peace with you?

She approaches JAMIE. *They straddle the past and present.*

Jamie Gillis?

Silence.

I'm sorry, Jamie Gillis.

Silence.

For all the things I said. That was wrong.

JAMIE *says nothing.*

Any word from your mother?

JAMIE *shakes his head.*

What about your dad?

JAMIE *shakes his head.*

He's coming home soon, Jamie. And he's gonna have a big load of lobsters on deck and we'll run to meet him.

JAMIE *digs and wipes away a tear. And there are tears in her eyes too.*

And until then you're coming to stay with us at my house. Okay? Cuz there's no point in having a war right here in Pugwash, is there?

He looks up at her, shakes his head no.

They look up.

JAMIE: Will ya look at that sunset, Conni McPhee?
Just *look.*
Have you ever seen such a beautiful thing?

She gets down into the sand.

And they build a castle.

Together.

Fin.

AFTERWORD

I don't envy anyone trying to explain via art what happened during a few days in July 1957 when a critical mass of scientists from around the world descended on the small town of Pugwash, Nova Scotia. There was indeed magic in the sunsets, or the water, or the lobster. Something happened there that changed trajectories.

The international scientists who met in Pugwash found a common language in science. They believed that once the dangers of the nuclear age were understood, leaders would change course. They reached across iron walls and put their own reputations on the line. In doing so they helped carve a path away from the nuclear abyss. Treaty by treaty, meeting by meeting, they injected new ways of thinking into an international system that had become mired in suspicion. They promoted a vision of a world free of nuclear weapons.

And yet here we are.

We are today living in very dangerous times, when some of the main accomplishments of the Pugwash scientists and their like-minded peers are under attack. When other threats to the planet are being ignored. When science itself is being sidelined and our daily sources of news are untrustworthy. When young people are trying to protect their future and world leaders are mocking them. (This hopefully will backfire. Don't mess with the kids, as Eaton warns in this play.)

Pugwash is a story ripe for retelling in as many different ways as we can, because at its heart is a universal and too often misunderstood call to "remember our humanity and forget the rest," as echoed from the 1955 Russell–Einstein Manifesto that led to the first meeting. That this unlikely meeting of some of the world's leading scientists took place in a remote corner of the world and gave rise to what became known as the Pugwash Conferences on Science and World Affairs remains a tale deserving to be told and retold. It's a story of courage, commitment, and a belief that there are ways to bridge our divides.

I was surprised and pleased that this play focused on children—imperfect, impressionable young people with their own dreams, their own very real fears, and their own limited experience. To me, that is its strength. Perhaps I am biased—my own introduction to the scientists of the Pugwash movement was as a student. I have known some of those scientists who were at the first meeting that gave birth to the Pugwash Conferences on Science and World Affairs. And what rings true in this play is their desire to reach across the generations. They knew well that their work was urgent. They literally feared universal death could result from a continuation of the nuclear arms race. Hundreds of Pugwash meetings have happened since then. They still gather today in some of the world's nuclear hotspots. The full story of Pugwash is not yet written because it is on going.

My dad used to say I had "last-word-itis." But it's actually a bit daunting to write an afterword to this play. Vern Thiessen has taken us back in time to encourage us to imagine how it must have been to have world affairs play out in a small town with its own history, and among townspeople with their own perspectives. I have since my own student days served in other roles in the Pugwash Conferences. I have written reports from

Pugwash meetings. I know all too well the precision that is brought to every word in a Pugwash statement. I suspect the scientists might have taken issue with some of the creative licences taken by the author (especially the implication that Eaton chaired the meetings, because to them it was integral that this was a meeting of and by scientists), but not with the play's intent or tone. It humanizes the participants. It makes one think of all those small moments that we don't see in the final reports. It shows the complexity of the many interpersonal interactions that would have unfolded over those days.

This play helps one imagine how complicated the experience must have been for each person, as every individual involved was on their own personal journey.

This play shows the symbiosis of the "Thinkers" and the town itself. We are not talking about a modern kind of conference where people fly to a high-end hotel and then leave. It was a trek and a half to get to Pugwash back then. There was no hotel large enough to house all the participants. They had no option but to interact with the townspeople. For scientists to meet to discuss their role in policy was a huge act of courage at that time. There were elements that were working against the intent of these scientists, as hinted in this play with the presence of a not-so-independent journalist. If the people of Pugwash had not opened their minds and their hearts to this experiment, then it would have failed. Of that there is no doubt. Cyrus Eaton fully understood the importance and the risks he took in extending the invitation to host this meeting at Thinkers' Lodge. He had great faith in Pugwash the town.

One of the men not featured in this play was Joseph Rotblat, the Polish-born physicist who quit the Manhattan Project—which developed the world's first nuclear weapons—on moral grounds. Rotblat was himself the new kid on the block—he was the youngest signatory of the Russell–Einstein Manifesto. He was integral to the success of first Pugwash Conference and the decades of work thereafter that culminated in the 1995 Nobel Peace Prize being jointly awarded to himself and to the organization he founded and led through some of the stormiest days of the Cold War. Rotblat's Nobel medal now hangs in Thinkers' Lodge, which has since been named a national historic site for the events that transpired there.

Joseph Rotblat had faith in the future. He and other "Pugwashites"—as the scientists of the Pugwash Conferences are known—envisioned not only a world without nuclear weapons but also a world without war. They believed that the same science that created the ability to destroy this beautiful planet also provided ways to bring us together and solve our problems.

The scientists concluded the report of what became known as the First Pugwash Conference with these words, "We are all convinced that mankind must abolish war or suffer catastrophe; that the dilemma of opposing power groups and the arms race must be broken; and that the establishment of lasting peace will mark the opening of a new and triumphant epoch for the whole of mankind. We earnestly hope that our conference may make a modest contribution to these great aims."

Surely now is a perfect time for a play like this, with a message like this, to reach across generations and across our own prejudices to remind us of our humanity and that vision of a better world. For that we must all thank Vern Thiessen for his contribution in bringing to life these small moments in the grand backdrop of a critical time in our history.

Sandra Ionno Butcher
Former Executive Director
Pugwash Conferences on Science and World Affairs

ACKNOWLEDGEMENTS

I am indebted to Ensemble Studio Theatre Artistic Director William Carden and Artistic Associate Graeme Gillis for pushing me to continue writing this play when, at times, I just wanted to give up. Ensemble Studio Theatre is the birthplace, playground, and finishing school of so many great playwrights. I am honoured to be a member of that company. Also thanks to Dr. Gabriel Cwilich for his insights and help. I am deeply thankful to Natasha MacLellan, Artistic Producer at Ship's Company Theatre in Parrsboro, Nova Scotia, for premiering the play.

I also owe a debt to the many archives, documentaries, newspaper articles, radio and TV interviews, and documents that I have liberally stolen from. These resources are all, to my knowledge, in the public domain. In particular the Mike Wallace interview that was recorded with Cyrus Eaton was highly illuminating. Vivian Godfree at the Pugwash archives helped me considerably, and I owe her a special thanks.

Thanks also to John Eaton, Cathy Eaton, Vivian and Jeremy Godfree, Paolo Brenciaglia, Chris Mullaley, Audrey MacPherson, Roger Mundle, Terry Smith, Evan Gillis, Allison Gillis, Nellie and John Van der Wiel, Denis Brown, Thelma Colborne, Wayne Arsenault, Ethel Langille Ingram, and Don Ingram. Also thanks to Paul and Jackie DeVries, Audrey

McLaughlin, and the participants of the 2012 Canada Pugwash Conferences, who allowed me to attend their sessions as a guest. Thanks also to my nephew Christopher Watters for assisting me with the physics. Also thanks to all the actors who participated in various workshops. And thanks to my wife, Susie Moloney, who read every draft and who, as always, is my biggest fan and best critic. And finally, thanks to two girls I met briefly in 2012, but who both deeply influenced me: Billie and Anneka. I saw them make art, and because of that, I wrote a play.

Vern Thiessen is one of Canada's most produced playwrights. His work has been seen across Canada, the United States, Europe, and Asia. He has been produced off-Broadway five times. Vern is the recipient of numerous awards, including the Dora Mavor Moore and Elizabeth Sterling Haynes Awards for Outstanding New Play, the Carol Bolt Award, the Gwen Pharis Ringwood Award, the City of Edmonton Arts Achievement Award, the University of Alberta Alumni Award of Excellence, and the Governor General's Literary Award for Drama, Canada's highest honour for a playwright.

First edition: December 2019
Printed and bound in Canada by Rapido Books, Montreal

Jacket art and design by Patrick Gray

PLAYWRIGHTS
CANADA PRESS
202-269 Richmond St. W.
Toronto, ON
M5V 1X1

416.703.0013
info@playwrightscanada.com
www.playwrightscanada.com
@playcanpress